# WHO CAME FIRST?

## NEW CLUES TO PREHISTORIC AMERICANS

### PATRICIA LAUBER

**NATIONAL GEOGRAPHIC**
Washington, D.C.

*I wish to thank Dr. Douglas W. Owsley,*
*Curator of Anthropology at the National*
*Museum of Natural History, Smithsonian*
*Institution, for his generous assistance and*
*helpful comments on the manuscript.*
*— P. L.*

Library of Congress Cataloging-in-Publication Data

Lauber, Patricia.
Who Came First? New Clues to Prehistoric Americans / by Patricia Lauber.
p. cm.
Includes bibliographical references and index.
Summary: Presents recent archaeological findings about the first people to settle the Americas, how they got here, and from what continents they came.
ISBN 0-7922-8228-0 (hardcover)
1. Indians—Origin—Juvenile literature. 2. America—Antiquities—Juvenile literature. [1. Indians—Origin. 2. America—Antiquities 3. Archaeology.] I. Title.
E61 .L348 2003          970.01—dc21
2002005278


Printed in Belgium

**PUBLISHED BY THE**
**NATIONAL GEOGRAPHIC SOCIETY**

John M. Fahey, Jr.
*President and Chief Executive Officer*

Gilbert M. Grosvenor
*Chairman of the Board*

Nina D. Hoffman
*Executive Vice President,*
*President of Books & Education*
*Publishing Group*

**STAFF FOR THIS BOOK**

Ericka Markman,
*Senior Vice President,*
*President of Children's Books*
*& Education Publishing Group*

Nancy Laties Feresten
*Vice President,*
*Editor-in-Chief of Children's Books*

Bea Jackson
*Art Director, Children's Books*

Jo Tunstall
*Project Editor*

David M. Seager
*Designer*

Melissa G. Ryan, Jo Tunstall, & Janet Dustin
*Illustrations Editors*

Janet Dustin
*Illustrations Coordinator*

Carl Mehler
*Director of Maps*

Martin Walz
*Map Production*

Jim Enzinna
*Indexing*

R. Gary Colbert
*Production Director*

Lewis R. Bassford
*Production Manager*

Vincent P. Ryan
*Manufacturing Manager*

*Front and Back Covers:*
Background, an 11,200-year-old wall painting from Pedra Pintada cave, located in the Brazilian Amazon. Points, from left to right (the same four points are repeated across the band):
Cactus Hill point, Clovis point, triangular point from Monte Alegre in the Brazilian Amazon, and Mesa point from Alaska.

*Front Cover:*
Skull of 9,500-year-old Kennewick Man, found along the Columbia River in Washington State.

*Points and Illustrations Used*
*in Chapter and Section Headings*:
Page 5, Clovis point; page 11, Cactus Hill point; page 27, Solutrean point from southwestern Europe; page 37, Haskett point; page 45, Mesa point from Alaska; page 53, computer-generated images of the skull and head of Kennewick Man; page 55, Fell's Cave point; page 60, Meadowcroft point.

*Page 63:*
Clovis spears with a spear shaft lying across them.

# C O N T E N T S

CHAPTER ONE

5

# A SURPRISING DISCOVERY

ON A SUMMER DAY IN 1996, TWO YOUNG men were wading along the edge of the Columbia River near Kennewick, Washington. One hit his foot on something hard and round.

It was a human skull.

The young men notified the police. The police gave the skull to the medical examiner. The appearance of the bones suggested that the skull was old. And so the medical examiner turned to Dr. James Chatters, a scientist known for his studies of ancient bones.

At first glance Dr. Chatters thought the skull had to be that of a white person, because it was not the right shape to be the skull of a Native American. Dr. Chatters thought the skull might have been that of a pioneer or a fur trapper.

THE KENNEWICK SKULL (LEFT) HAD SEVERAL TRAITS THAT MADE IT LOOK EUROPEAN: A DELICATE JAW; A LONG, NARROW HEAD; THE ANGLE BETWEEN FOREHEAD AND NOSE. DR. CHATTERS (RIGHT) WORKS ON A CAST OF THE KENNEWICK MAN SKULL, USING WAX TO BUILD UP THE MISSING PORTIONS.

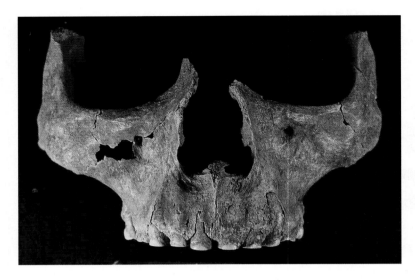

A DIET OF COARSE FOODS WORE DOWN THE TEETH OF EARLY PEOPLES, AND IT WORE DOWN KENNEWICK MAN'S (ABOVE). STARTING WITH A CAST OF THE SKULL, A SCULPTOR MADE A MODEL OF WHAT HE THOUGHT KENNEWICK MAN HAD LOOKED LIKE (RIGHT). NO ONE KNOWS WHETHER KENNEWICK MAN HAD A BEARD OR WHAT HIS HAIR WAS LIKE, SO NEITHER WAS ADDED.

But a closer look showed something odd. The teeth were worn flat, as they often are in the skulls of early peoples. Dr. Chatters decided to look for the rest of the skeleton. A search along the river turned up nearly all the bones.

Once the bones were laid out in his laboratory, Dr. Chatters' first job was to discover their sex, age, and race. Race was important. If the bones were those of a Native American, they would have to be returned to their tribe. That was the law.

Bones showed that the skeleton was that of a man—Kennewick Man, as he came to be called. Bones and teeth showed that Kennewick Man had died between the ages of 40 and 55. He had some broken ribs and arthritis but otherwise appeared to have been in good health. Dr. Chatters said he was "Caucasoid." This is the term for a large group of people who share certain traits, such as a long, narrow brain case and a narrow face. The group takes in Europeans and some peoples of southern Asia.

Then he got a big surprise.

Something was lodged in the bone just above one hip. It proved to be part of a stone spear point. The point had had the shape of a willow leaf and was a kind widely used in the

Pacific Northwest 9,500 to 6,000 years ago. Clearly, Kennewick Man had not been a pioneer or a fur trapper.

A tiny bone was sent to a laboratory for dating. It proved to be some 9,500 years old. With this discovery, the puzzle deepened. Was Kennewick Man an ancestor of today's Native Americans? Or could he be someone else?

For scientists who study early Americans, this was the most important find in years. The bones of Kennewick Man are among the oldest known in the Americas, and such bones are rare. Scientists know of only seven other American skeletons that are equally well preserved and dated.

Tests of his bones showed that Kennewick Man was an eater of fish—perhaps he was a fisherman. He was tall for a man of his time—five feet nine inches—slim, well built, with even features. He still had all his teeth, and none of them had cavities.

Kennewick Man was probably part of a small band of people who moved about, hunting, fishing, and gathering plant foods. The people of his time had fine

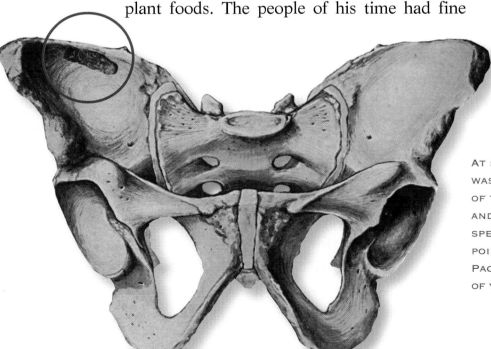

AT SOME TIME KENNEWICK MAN WAS INJURED BY A SPEAR. PART OF THE STONE POINT BROKE OFF AND LODGED IN HIS HIP. THE SPEAR POINT WAS A CASCADE POINT, A KIND USED IN THE PACIFIC NORTHWEST THOUSANDS OF YEARS AGO.

IN THE TIME OF KENNEWICK
MAN, PEOPLE MOVED ABOUT
IN SMALL BANDS, HUNTING
AND GATHERING FOOD OF
VARIOUS KINDS.

sewing needles made of bone, and so he would have tailored clothing and lived in a tent. He may or may not have been buried in a grave. It's possible that he died alone, on or near the river, perhaps swept away by a flood and buried under sand until the river uncovered his bones.

A brief time was all that Dr. Chatters had with Kennewick Man. Once his age became known, five Indian tribes claimed him as an ancestor. They wanted to return him to the earth, as their religious beliefs demanded. The government agreed that the bones should be turned over to the Indians. To stop this from happening, a group of scientists sued the government, saying it had not followed the law—it had not shown that Kennewick Man was a Native American. Until the matter could be settled, the bones were stored in a museum.

The scientists wanted the bones for study. They knew that Kennewick Man still had much to tell them about the peopling of the Americas. The bones are part of new evidence that raises questions about a mystery many scientists thought they had solved years ago.

# HOW CARBON-14 DATING IS DONE

Archaeologists and anthropologists have several ways to date their ancient finds. One of the most useful is a built-in atomic clock called carbon 14, which was first used in the 1950s. It is found in once living things such as wood, charcoal, shells, bones, seeds.

Carbon 14 forms in the atmosphere, several miles above the surface of the Earth. It is radioactive. That is, its atoms keep breaking down or decaying—they give off small parts of themselves. When carbon 14 combines with oxygen

in the air, it forms radioactive carbon dioxide, which mixes with other carbon dioxide in the air.

Green plants take in carbon dioxide, which they use in making their food. And so each plant holds a tiny amount of carbon 14. Animals eat plants or eat plant eaters. And so every animal also holds a tiny amount of carbon 14. The carbon 14 keeps decaying, but more keeps being added.

When a plant or animal dies, it stops taking in carbon 14. The amount it already has, though,

goes on decaying. It does so at a steady rate. After about 5,600 years, half the carbon-14 atoms have changed to nitrogen through the process of radioactive decay; half are left. After another 5,600 years, half of the half has broken down, and so on.

Scientists can measure the amount of carbon 14 left in a sample of something that was once living. This is their atomic clock. It tells them how much time has passed since the plant or animal died—how old it is. It's as if you had set a kitchen timer for 30 minutes and someone tells you it will ring in 5. You then know it has been running for 25 minutes.

Carbon 14 is used for dating things that are no more than 40,000 to 50,000 years old. After that, little carbon 14 is left.

Although carbon 14 breaks down at a steady rate, it does not build up at a steady rate. And so carbon-14 years are not exactly the same as calendar years. Scientists usually use radiocarbon, or carbon-14, years, but these dates can be changed into calendar years.

Dates in this book are given in calendar years.

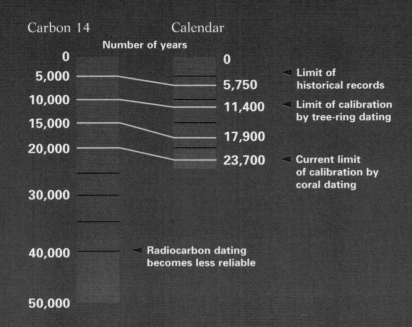

Carbon 14     Calendar

**Number of years**

| Carbon 14 | Calendar | |
|---|---|---|
| 0 | 0 | |
| 5,000 | 5,750 | ◄ Limit of historical records |
| 10,000 | 11,400 | ◄ Limit of calibration by tree-ring dating |
| 15,000 | 17,900 | |
| 20,000 | 23,700 | ◄ Current limit of calibration by coral dating |
| 30,000 | | |
| 40,000 | | ◄ Radiocarbon dating becomes less reliable |
| 50,000 | | |

# THE MYSTERY

**W**HEN EUROPEAN EXPLORERS CROSSED the Atlantic Ocean, they came to a world that was new to them: the two continents that we call the Americas. They also found a big puzzle: People were living in these lands. They were not the East Indians, Chinese, or Japanese that the first explorers expected. Who were they? Had they always lived in this new world? If not, where had they come from—and when and how? The more that Europeans learned about the people, whom they called Indians, the deeper the mystery became.

The Indians were spread through both continents—from coast to coast and from the far north to the tip of South America. No two groups seemed alike. The Indians Columbus met on his first landfall in the Caribbean were peace-loving fishermen. On neighboring islands the Indians were warriors and cannibals.

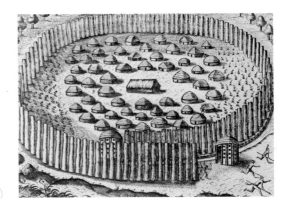

EUROPEAN EXPLORERS WERE SURPRISED BY THE VARIETY OF INDIAN CULTURES THEY ENCOUNTERED. THESE PICTURES WERE DRAWN IN THE 1500S BY A MEMBER OF A FRENCH EXPEDITION TO WHAT IS NOW THE SOUTH-EASTERN UNITED STATES. THE ENGRAVING (ABOVE) SHOWS A FORTIFIED INDIAN VILLAGE. THE PAINTING AT LEFT SHOWS HOW ONE TRIBE CELEBRATED ESCAPES FROM GREAT DANGER, WHETHER AT SEA OR ON LAND.

In the Southwest, Indians lived in villages and farmed irrigated fields. On the Great Plains, they lived by hunting and gathering. In the eastern woodlands, Indians hunted, fished, and farmed.

The most surprising discoveries were made in Mexico, Guatemala, and Peru. Here Europeans found two great civilizations in full bloom: the Aztec in Mexico and the Inca in Peru. In Guatemala and southern Mexico they found the ruins of the once great Maya civilization.

European scholars of the time were greatly puzzled. How could these Indians be accounted for? Over the years many answers were suggested. None really worked.

Finally, in the 1930s, scientists thought they had solved the puzzle. They pieced together some important discoveries they had made. Parts of the puzzle were still missing, but the scientists could guess what those pieces might be like. The solution they worked out was a theory—an idea based on evidence.

The first Americans, they said, were a people who came from Siberia. They were northern Asians. They arrived at a time when Siberia and Alaska were linked by land, during the Ice Age. In an ice age, heavy snows fall on polar lands and mountaintops, more than the summer sun can melt. Over hundreds or thousands of years, the snows build up. Under the weight of new

Modern island shoreline

Ice Age island shoreline

Glacier

TODAY'S GLACIERS (RIGHT) ARE REMINDERS OF MILE-THICK SHEETS OF ICE THAT ONCE COVERED NOW GREEN LANDS. IN THE ICE AGE, WHEN HUGE AMOUNTS OF WATER WERE LOCKED UP ON LAND AS ICE, OCEAN LEVELS FELL AND NEW LAND APPEARED. WHEN THE GLACIERS MELTED, OCEAN LEVELS ROSE AGAIN (ABOVE).

snows, the old layers change to ice. And in time the ice begins to flow. A mile or more thick, it creeps out over the land. These great masses of ice are called glaciers or ice sheets.

Most of the water that falls as snow comes from the oceans. When snow melts, the water, sooner or later, runs back into the oceans. But when glaciers are growing, snow is not melting. A huge amount of ocean water becomes locked up on land as ice. Ocean levels drop by hundreds of feet. New land—land that was formerly covered by water—appears along the coasts.

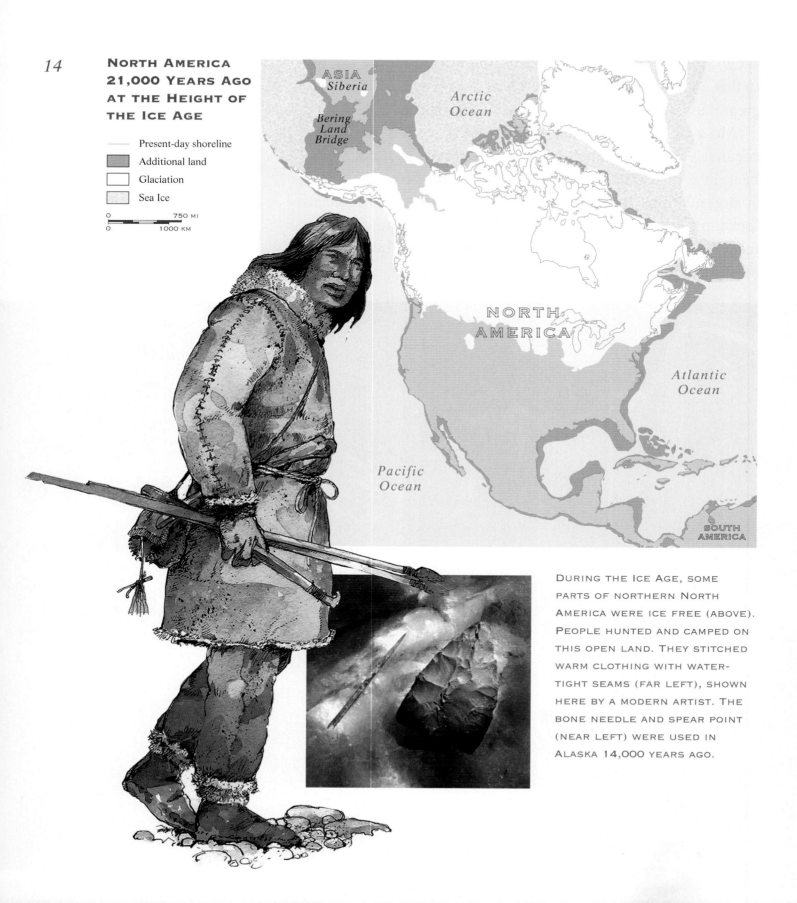

NORTH AMERICA
21,000 YEARS AGO
AT THE HEIGHT OF
THE ICE AGE

—— Present-day shoreline

Additional land

Glaciation

Sea Ice

0            750 MI
0          1000 KM

ASIA
*Siberia*

Bering
Land
Bridge

*Arctic
Ocean*

NORTH
AMERICA

*Pacific
Ocean*

*Atlantic
Ocean*

SOUTH
AMERICA

DURING THE ICE AGE, SOME
PARTS OF NORTHERN NORTH
AMERICA WERE ICE FREE (ABOVE).
PEOPLE HUNTED AND CAMPED ON
THIS OPEN LAND. THEY STITCHED
WARM CLOTHING WITH WATER-
TIGHT SEAMS (FAR LEFT), SHOWN
HERE BY A MODERN ARTIST. THE
BONE NEEDLE AND SPEAR POINT
(NEAR LEFT) WERE USED IN
ALASKA 14,000 YEARS AGO.

During part of the most recent ice age, North America and Asia were joined by land. Where an arm of Siberia reached toward an arm of Alaska, the shallow seas went dry. The seabeds formed a broad plain that stretched some 600 miles from north to south. This region is called either the Bering Land Bridge or Beringia. People from Siberia lived on this plain for hundreds or thousands of years. It must have been cold and raw. But people had bone needles, and they could stitch furs into clothing that was warm and watertight.

Many archaeologists and other scientists have long thought the first Americans reached Alaska from this land bridge. Traveling on foot, they said, bands of people entered a new world about 14,000 years ago. At that time, huge ice sheets covered much of Canada and Alaska, reaching south of what is now the border between Canada and the United States. One glacier spread from east to west. The other spread from west to east.

Scientists thought that an ice-free corridor lay between the two big sheets of ice. The people moved south through the corridor to the Great Plains. From there they spread out.

In the early 1930s, archaeologists were studying a people they had named Folsom after the place in New Mexico where their tools were first found. Folsom people were big-game hunters, the earliest known in the Americas. The archaeologists were looking for more traces of them near Clovis, New Mexico.

In Ice Age times, the area around Clovis was a lake-dotted, grassy grazing ground for herds of big mammals. Archaeologists could see that Clovis had been a good place to hunt because they found large numbers of mammoth, bison, and camel bones. They could also see that people had hunted here over a long period of time, because the bones and stone points were found in layers. This is what happens

THE SIDE WALL OF THIS DIG HAS BEEN CAREFULLY TAGGED BY ARCHAEOLOGISTS TO MARK THE LAYERS THAT WERE LAID DOWN OVER CENTURIES.

when generation after generation of people live in one place. The first generation loses things. It throws away whatever it doesn't want, such as bones and broken tools. These things get mixed with dust, dirt, stones, and rotting plant matter. On top of this layer is what the next generation loses or throws away. And so, over time, layers build up, with the most recent on top and the oldest at the bottom.

As the archaeologists at Clovis dug down, they made a great discovery. They came on beautifully crafted stone spear points that had not been made by Folsom men, but by even earlier hunters. They named this people and their culture Clovis. Since then, traces of Clovis have been found in many parts of North America.

Clovis spear points were sometimes found in the bones of mastodons and mammoths, and so the people were thought

ARCHAEOLOGISTS WERE LOOKING FOR FOLSOM POINTS (NEAR RIGHT) AND OTHER TOOLS WHEN THEY CAME UPON TRACES OF AN EARLIER PEOPLE WHO HAD CRAFTED BEAUTIFUL SPEAR POINTS (FAR RIGHT AND BELOW). THESE PEOPLE WERE LATER NAMED CLOVIS.

HUNTERS FIRST ATTACKED MAMMOTHS AND MASTODONS WITH ATLATLS, SMALL
SPEARS LAUNCHED WITH THROWING STICKS (ABOVE). MOVING IN FOR THE KILL,
THEY USED THRUSTING SPEARS (LEFT). MASTODON MOLARS HAVE CONE-LIKE
POINTS, SUITED TO CRUSHING COARSE PLANT FOOD. THE TOOTH BELOW IS
SHOWN ACTUAL SIZE AND WAS FOUND IN KANSAS.

of as big-game hunters. They had the skills and the weapons to hunt a Columbian mammoth, which stood 13 feet high at the shoulder, weighed eight tons, and could probably run 25 miles an hour. When attacked, it defended itself with tusks and head— slashing and battering. The hunters had two weapons. One was an atlatl, a small spear launched with a throwing stick. The other was a thrusting spear, used for close-in work. Both were tipped with leaf-shaped, sharp-edged points five to six inches long. The points were beautifully designed and made from only certain kinds of stone. They were tools, but they were also works of art.

The Clovis culture first appeared in North America about 13,500 years ago. It appeared suddenly. No one has ever found early, crude Clovis points, the kind of work people might do while learning to make beautiful points. After about 500 years, Clovis culture disappeared just as

suddenly as it had appeared. No one knows why. In its place tools and weapons made in other styles appear.

For 70 years, most archaeologists believed that the mystery of the first Americans had been solved. They knew there were northern Asian people in Siberia during the Ice Age. They knew there was a way for these people to reach North America by land—over the Bering Land Bridge. They knew that Clovis tools had been found all across North America. They fitted these pieces together and said that Clovis people, northern Asians from Siberia, were the first to colonize the Americas. The evidence for Clovis was there. It was widespread. It was definite.

Yet there have always been problems with the theory that Clovis came first and all other groups descended from them. For one thing, the Indians that explorers found did not appear to be a single people. They spoke many languages and had many cultures. They did not necessarily look alike. The members of one tribe might be tall, while those of another tribe might have short legs.

THIS CLOVIS TOOL KIT INCLUDED SCRAPERS, BLADES, POUNDERS, SPEAR POINTS. WHAT APPEARS TO BE A WRENCH (LEFT CENTER AND ABOVE) WAS MADE OF BONE AND MOST LIKELY USED TO STRAIGHTEN SPEAR SHAFTS.

Another problem has to do with the two big glaciers in Canada. There is no way people could cross that much ice on foot, no way they could feed themselves. That is why, archaeologists said, there must have been a passageway. How else could these people have reached the Great Plains? But the ice-free corridor may never have existed. Not long ago geologists looked for traces of it. They knew where it should have been. And they reasoned that an ice-free corridor would have had plants and animals if people could migrate through it. So there should be traces of these plants and animals in the corridor—if it existed. The geologists found the remains of animals that lived in the area from 40,000 to 21,000 years ago, when the two glaciers met. For the next 10,000 years no animals lived in the area.

Still another problem has to do with speed. Moving on foot over a few hundred years, Clovis people seem to have reached far-flung areas. Their spear points are found from California to Virginia and from the south-

MODERN REPRODUCTIONS SHOW HOW CLOVIS SPEAR POINTS WERE FITTED, OR HAFTED, TO THEIR SHAFTS.

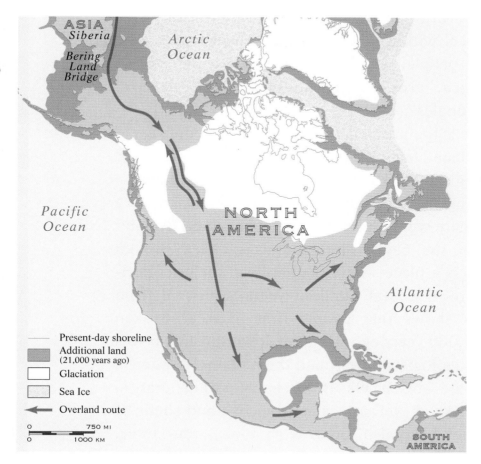

BY 11,000 TO 10,000 YEARS AGO, THE GREAT CANADIAN GLACIERS WERE
MELTING AND SHRINKING. A PASSAGEWAY HAD OPENED BETWEEN THEM,
OFFERING AN OVERLAND ROUTE BETWEEN NORTH AND SOUTH.

ern edges of the glaciers into Mexico. If Clovis people also
settled South America, they traveled 10,000 miles to do so.

It is hard to understand why a people would do this in an
uncrowded land. They had only dogs as pack animals—they
had no horses or oxen. They had not invented the wheel.
They had to carry belongings and babies. Travel must have
been hard and slow.

Also, there was no one to tell them anything when they
spread into a new region. Moving meant finding new sources

24  of water, discovering which plants were safe to eat, learning how to deal with a new climate. With plenty of land and no local people, why would they go to the end of South America, crossing mountains, rivers, deserts, forests, and jungles?

Then there is the problem of where Clovis people came from. If they came from Siberia, there should be traces of them there and in Alaska. So far no one has found any.

Even during the Ice Age, some parts of Alaska were free of ice. There were places where people could live and hunt. One of the oldest sites found is called Broken Mammoth. It is a place where people lived for brief periods of time over several hundred years. Charcoal from their hearths shows that people first lived at Broken Mammoth 14,000 years ago. Digging down through layers of earth, archaeologists have found the remains of animals these people ate—bison, elk, foxes, hares, swans, cranes, geese, and ducks as well as scales from fish and shells of bird eggs. They have also found ivory tools, stone tools, stone flakes, and what appear to be spear points. But the tools and points are not those of Clovis.

Still another problem has to do with finds that appear to be older than Clovis. Some of these are in North America and some are in South America. They are a big challenge to the Clovis-first theory.

ANIMAL BONES FOUND AT BROKEN MAMMOTH SHOW THAT THE PEOPLE ATE A VARIETY OF ANIMALS, AMONG THEM SEABIRDS. CARIBOU, AND MOOSE.

# CHAPTER THREE

# SEARCHING FOR SOUTH AMERICAN SETTLERS

**M**ONTE VERDE, IN SOUTH-CENTRAL CHILE, is one of the oldest sites found so far. It was dug over several years by scientists led by Dr. Thomas D. Dillehay of the University of Kentucky. He thinks that nearly 15,000 years ago, 30 or more people lived at Monte Verde for about a year. For shelter they had huts or tents made of hides. They had two big hearths where large pieces of meat could be cooked. They also had small cooking pots lined with clay, which held burning charcoal. The bones of seven different mastodons were found near one hut that was set apart from the others, perhaps as a place for butchering. The bones are one sign that the site is old. Mastodons died out about 13,000 years ago.

SCIENTISTS EXPLORE THE ANCIENT SITE OF MONTE VERDE, IN CHILE (LEFT). THEY WERE TRYING TO VERIFY ITS AGE. AMONG THE FINDS THAT DR. DILLEHAY AND HIS TEAM (ABOVE RIGHT) MADE WAS A CHUNK OF MASTODON MEAT PRESERVED IN A PEAT BOG.

AT MONTE VERDE A SMALL
HUMAN FOOTPRINT WAS
FOUND IN THE CLAY BESIDE
A FIRE PIT.

AMONG THE OBJECTS FOUND
AT MONTE VERDE WERE A
DIGGING STICK, WHICH
WORKED LIKE A CROWBAR;
KNOTTED REED TWINE, WHICH
BOUND TWO TIMBERS TOGETHER;
CHARRED MASTODON RIBS,
WHICH WERE PROBABLY USED
AS FIRE POKERS.

Archaeologists found traces of 45 food plants, such as wild potatoes and mushrooms. Some did not grow locally but came from mountains called the Andes or the coast, up to 150 miles away. The people must have roamed widely or traded with other groups. Archaeologists also found 22 kinds of medicinal plants that are still used by local people. These plants are a sign that the ancient people were not newcomers. It takes time to learn which plants can be used for medicine.

The Monte Verde settlement came to a sudden end. And that is probably why we know about it. The water table rose, flooding the settlement and forcing the people to move. After a while, mosses grew over the water. They died, sank, and were replaced by more mosses. As this happened over and over again, a peat bog formed. It sealed the settlement under a kind of cap, preserving traces of the people who had

lived there. Monte Verde is one of the few sites where materials such as wood and hides have not wholly rotted away. There are no human bones, but preserved in clay near a hearth is a small footprint, probably made by a child.

Other traces of the people are planks and stakes, grinding bowls, digging sticks, a pointed spear, and what may be tent pegs. The stone tools are simple. Some seem to have been shaped naturally. Some were shaped by human hands. None look like Clovis tools and weapons.

LLAMA-LIKE ANIMALS WERE AMONG THE LARGE PREY HUNTED IN SOUTH AMERICA. HUNTERS OF BIG GAME WERE PROBABLY MEN, BUT MEN, WOMEN, AND CHILDREN TRAPPED SMALL GAME AND GATHERED FRUITS, NUTS, ROOTS, AND OTHER PLANT FOODS, AS SHOWN IN THIS DRAWING BY A MODERN ARTIST.

**SOME EARLY SOUTH AMERICAN SITES**

Legend on map:
- Early American sites
- Present-day shoreline
- Present-day political boundaries
- Additional land (21,000 years ago)

0 — 750 MI
0 — 1000 KM

Map labels: NORTH AMERICA, TAIMA-TAIMA, VENEZUELA, TIBITÓ, COLOMBIA, Amazon River, PEDRA PINTADA, SOUTH AMERICA, TOCA DO PEDRA FURADA, PERU, BRAZIL, PACHAMACHAY, LAPA DO BOQUÊTE, QUEBRADA TACAHUAY, LAPA VERMELHA, Pacific Ocean, Atlantic Ocean, ARGENTINA, CHILE, MONTE VERDE, LOS TOLDOS, Río Pinturas, PIEDRA MUSEO, TRES ARROYOS, TÚNEL, Atlantic Ocean

Another site is just 200 feet away. Here scientists have found simple tools, one of which had traces of mastodon blood. They have found what appear to be hearths with charcoal. Carbon-14 dating has given an age of 33,000 years for the charcoal. But so far no one has proved that the charcoal came from a fire made by humans.

In northeast Brazil there is a site called Pedra Furada, which also appears to be very old. It is a rock shelter at the foot of a high sandstone cliff. Sandstone is soft rock. As it weathered over the years, tiny pieces wore off, fell to the floor of the shelter, and built up in layers. Dr. Niéde Guidon, a French-Brazilian archaeologist, and her team spent ten years digging through 16 feet of layers. They found some 600 simple stone tools and charcoal from ancient fires. Dates for some of the charcoal appear to go back at least 32,000 years.

Other sites have been found in South America that seem to be about the same age as Clovis. They show bands of people were living in all kinds of places in South America—along the coasts, high in the Andes Mountains, in deserts, grasslands, woodlands, rain forests. The people in each area had their own ways of gathering and catching food, of making simple tools.

Some people were even in the Amazon Basin of Brazil, a place where scientists thought the first Americans could not make a living, because Clovis people were big-game hunters who lived in open areas with mild climates. In the hot, wet tropics, large animals were scarce. No one could live there, the scientists said, until people developed farming thousands of years later.

HUNTERS IN SOUTH AMERICA USED WHIRLING STONES TO BRING DOWN LARGE PREY, AS SHOWN IN THIS MODERN DRAWING. THE PHOTOGRAPH SHOWS A REPRODUCTION OF A STONE AND THE REED TWINE USED TO MAKE A SLING.

PEDRA PINTADA, A CAVE ON THE NORTH BANK OF THE AMAZON RIVER IN BRAZIL, YIELDED CAVE PAINTINGS, SPEAR POINTS, AND OTHER EVIDENCE INDICATING THAT PEOPLE LIVED THERE AT THE TIME OF CLOVIS.

But early people did live there. They used a cave in a sandstone cliff, Pedra Pintada, which is near the present-day town of Monte Alegre. The cave was known to local people because it had paintings on its walls. Several archaeologists said the paintings must be modern because ancient people could not have lived here. One, Dr. Anna Roosevelt of the University of Illinois, decided to find out by digging. She and her fellow workers found evidence that people were living in the cave at the time of Clovis—but they were not Clovis big-game hunters.

These people made spear points that were the shape of triangles on stems. The large number of stone flakes found is a sign that the people spent much time making or repairing tools. They were hunters of small game. Their foods were fish, shellfish, small mammals, turtles, birds, fruits, and nuts. Bones show that some of the fish were five feet long. The length suggests that these people had boats or rafts and went out on the water to spear fish.

At least two sites in South America seem to be older than Clovis. A number of sites seem to be about the same age. If this is true, then South America could not have been colonized by Clovis people. Where did the people come from and how could they have reached South America, archaeologists wondered.

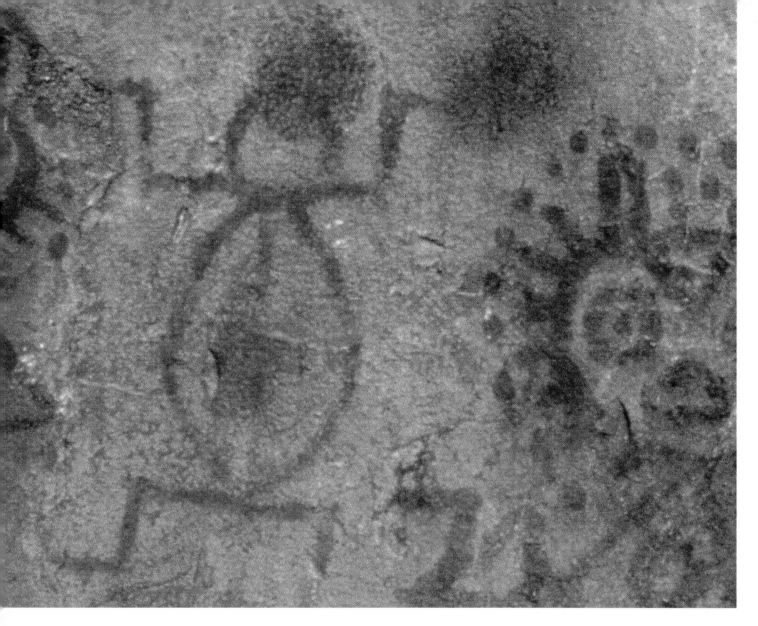

33

PEDRA PINTADA CAVE PAINTINGS SHOW HUMAN FIGURES (ABOVE), ANIMALS, GEOMETRIC DESIGNS. DISCOVERY IN THE CAVE OF TRIANGULAR SPEAR POINTS (LEFT) AND THE CHARRED REMAINS OF TREES AND ANIMALS TELLS OF AN EARLY HUNTER-GATHERER SOCIETY. DR. ROOSEVELT (NEAR LEFT) WORKS IN HER FOREST "OFFICE" IN BRAZIL.

There seemed to be only two answers. One was that they traveled by land, crossing from Siberia before the two great Canadian glaciers joined — perhaps 30,000 years ago. The other answer was that people from Asia arrived in boats, probably made of hides stretched over wooden frames.

Scientists know ancient peoples had boats. At least 50,000 years ago the first settlers reached Australia from Java. They must have traveled by boat — there was no other way to cross 80 miles of water.

Few scientists think that ancient peoples simply sailed across the Pacific and landed in South America. The Pacific is a very large and often stormy ocean. To cross it people would need to be skilled sailors. They would need to know how to find the way. Indeed, they would need to know that there was a way to find, that the ocean did not go on forever. They would need large supplies of food and water, enough for the hundred or so people who could form a colony — men, women, and children of different ages and skills.

A better route for people in boats would be along the coast. From northeast Asia, they could travel east, hugging the shore of Beringia, putting in for food, water, and rest from time to time. Then they could head down the west coast of North America. A sea route was possible at a time when glaciers blocked the land route. Travel by boat would be swift. People could easily cover long distances.

At one time scientists thought a sea route was impossible. There were no landing places, they said, because glaciers reached all the way to the edge of the Pacific Ocean. There was no place for people to go ashore for a while.

Now geologists have shown that there were ice-free pockets of land along the coast. People could have gone ashore. Food was plentiful — seals and other marine mammals, shellfish,

and fish. To feed themselves, people needed only fairly simple tools—nets, harpoons, clubs, knives. Also, as people traveled south, they could have gathered and eaten familiar foods from the sea. There would be no need to learn about new land plants.

Once they arrived, people probably would have first settled near the coast, then later followed the rivers inland.

A sea route is hard to prove. Materials such as hides and wood rot away. And there can be little trace of the ice-free pockets where people may have camped. When glaciers melted, sea levels rose hundreds of feet, and Ice Age coastlines disappeared.

Still, a sea route makes sense. And some finds support the idea—objects found off British Columbia, among islands off California, and off the coast of Peru.

Monte Verde and other South American sites have forced archaeologists to question earlier ideas and theories. They have also caused some scientists working in North America to dig deeper.

OFF THE COAST OF BRITISH COLUMBIA, CANADIAN ARCHAEOLOGIST DARYL FEDJE CLEANS MUD FROM ROCKS DREDGED FROM WHAT IS NOW THE SEAFLOOR BUT WAS A FOREST DURING THE ICE AGE. HE IS LOOKING FOR STONE TOOLS LIKE THE ONE HE FOUND IN 1998 ON WHAT MUST HAVE BEEN AN ICE AGE SHORELINE 11,500 YEARS AGO.

C H A P T E R   F O U R

# LOOKING AGAIN AT NORTH AMERICA

**F**OR MANY YEARS ARCHAEOLOGISTS WORKING in North America paid little attention to sites in South America. The finds were not what they expected and did not fit the Clovis-first theory. For the same reasons, they also ignored certain finds in North America. But work in South America seems to show that people lived there much earlier than expected. And so a number of scientists have taken a second look at some North American sites.

One of these is Meadowcroft Rockshelter, near Pittsburgh, Pennsylvania. Nearly 30 years ago, Dr. James Adovasio, now a professor at the Mercyhurst Archaeological Institute, and his

AT THE MEADOWCROFT ROCKSHELTER, DR. ADOVASIO (LEFT) AND HIS TEAM ARE CAREFUL TO RECORD EXACTLY WHERE EVERYTHING WAS FOUND. THE SPEAR POINT (RIGHT) WAS THE FIRST SIGN OF PEOPLE WHO HAD LIVED AT THE SITE BEFORE CLOVIS.

students began to dig in the floor of a sandstone overhang. It was a place where modern people had been building fires and camping out. Very likely, Dr. Adovasio thought, people had been using it for a long time. Traces of them would be buried in the sand that kept eroding from the overhanging rock.

The top layer yielded modern aluminum cans. A little lower were older cans, made of steel. The team dug past modern bottles and colonial bottles. They found traces of Indians who had made a fire and butchered a deer around 1320.

Digging on, they found traces of ancient people who had used the shelter. Dr. Adovasio really expected to stop making finds once he had reached the age of Clovis. But his team dug on—and found more and more. They found an unknown kind of spear point. They found fire pits. They found simple stone tools that were not made in the Clovis style. Carbon-14 dating gave the oldest charcoal a date of 20,000 years.

When Dr. Adovasio presented his findings, other scientists found fault with them and brushed them aside. The findings had to be wrong because Clovis was first.

But now there is also Cactus Hill, a campsite southeast of Richmond, Virginia, near the Nottoway River. When archaeologists dug two feet into sandy soil, they found tools made in the Clovis style, which proved to be 11,000 years old. When they dug deeper in the layers of sand, they found tools of a different style made from river stones. These looked much like the tools found at Meadowcroft. Along with the tools, archaeologists found charcoal that may be 18,000 years old, according to Dr. Joseph M. McAvoy, leader of the archaeological research team.

The earliest people to use Cactus Hill hunted small game, such as rabbits, and cooked over wood from pine trees. People went on living at Cactus Hill for thousands of years, probably because it was a good site—near the river but slightly raised and well drained.

There is also Topper, a site on the Savannah River in South Carolina. Digging here, Dr. Albert Goodyear, an archaeologist at the University of South Carolina, came upon a layer of Clovis tools. He dug a little farther and then stopped because he thought Clovis was the oldest he could find. But after thinking about Monte Verde, he decided that Topper might be a good place to look for people who were earlier than Clovis. Three feet deeper, he found earlier tools.

DR. MCAVOY AND HIS WIFE, LYNN, WORK AT CACTUS HILL. THEY FOUND TOOLS, SUCH AS THIS SPEAR POINT, THAT WERE OLDER THAN CLOVIS POINTS AND MADE IN A DIFFERENT STYLE.

40

STONE CHIPS AT THE PLACES WHERE EARLY PEOPLE LIVED SHOW THAT THEY SPENT MUCH TIME MAKING AND REPAIRING STONE TOOLS, AS SHOWN IN THIS MODERN DRAWING. THEY FEASTED ON MAMMOTH, CARIBOU, AND ELK THAT THEY KILLED WITH STONE SPEAR POINTS. BUT MANY SCIENTISTS THINK MOST MEALS WERE OF SMALL GAME—RABBITS, SQUIRRELS, TURTLES, AS WELL AS SEAFOOD AND WATER BIRDS. THESE WERE CAUGHT IN TRAPS, NETS, AND SNARES MADE OF WOOD AND FIBER, WHICH HAVE LONG SINCE ROTTED AWAY.

Today a number of scientists are ready to accept Meadowcroft, Cactus Hill, Topper, and Monte Verde. But others feel that these sites do not measure up. To be accepted, evidence must meet certain standards that archaeologists have agreed on:

■ The find must be human bones or objects made by human hands.

■ It must be buried in earth that has not later been disturbed by humans or by natural causes.

■ It must be found with good evidence of age, such as the bones of animals that have died out.

Over the years, many sites have failed to meet the standards. A great many things can go wrong.

Suppose charcoal is found next to a stone tool. The charcoal can be dated, but there may be no way to tell how it came to be in the cave. Perhaps an animal carried it in and the charcoal has nothing to do with the tool. It might even have come from a natural fire and not from one made by humans. Sometimes there is no way to tell—and no way to date the stone tool.

Scientists can make mistakes unless they are very careful to measure and record just where everything was found. Once digging begins, a site is forever changed. It can never be put back the way it was. To be of value, it must be carefully dug, mapped, and recorded.

In general, to dig deeper into the earth is to dig deeper into the past. But this is not always true. Ground may have been disturbed by an earthquake. Burrowing animals may have moved objects from one layer to another. A flood may have mixed up several layers.

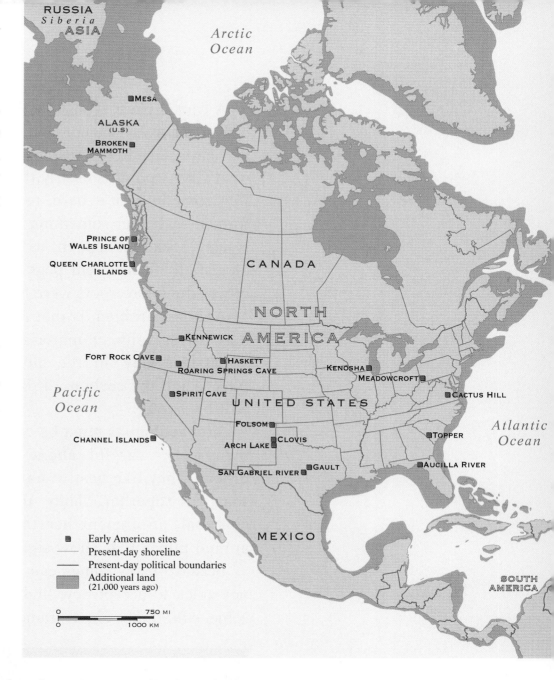

SOME EARLY
NORTH AMERICAN
SITES

A carved piece of mammoth ivory can be dated. But the date of the ivory may not be the date it was carved. The ivory may have come from a mammoth that died much earlier.

A Clovis point is clearly the work of a talented human. But sometimes it's hard to be sure how other things formed—whether something is an early tool or whether it is just a rock that happens to look like a tool. Some archaeologists think that tent pegs were found at Monte Verde; others think tree roots were found.

Another problem is that nearby older carbon material may affect younger material, much as dye from a red sweatshirt may, in the laundry, turn a white T-shirt pink. Then the carbon-14 date for the younger material will be wrong.

Archaeologists must be very careful—careful in their own work, careful about accepting the findings of others. They like best to have several kinds of evidence that fit together. They like, for example, to find charcoal, an ancient hearth, stone chips, and perhaps animal bones that show signs of butchering.

Because many things can go wrong, archaeologists are not quick to accept new findings. That is one reason why some still think Clovis came first. They are sure about

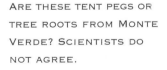

ARE THESE TENT PEGS OR TREE ROOTS FROM MONTE VERDE? SCIENTISTS DO NOT AGREE.

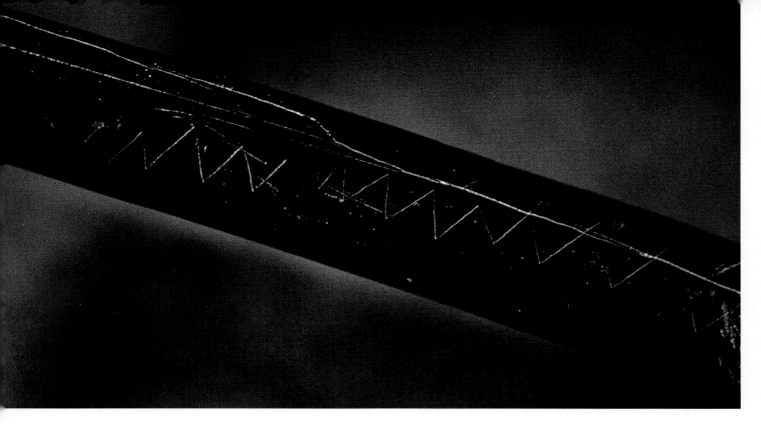

Clovis: the dates, the skills, the spread of the sites. But it is also true that most of these archaeologists have spent their lives working on Clovis. They can't easily give up the Clovis-first idea.

No one doubts that people crossed by land from Siberia. But when did they do it? Did they cross well before the two great glaciers grew together? Did some cross and stay in Alaska until a corridor south opened up? Did some come much later, as the Aleuts, Inuit, and some Indian groups did—coming by foot when the winter seas froze or paddling boats along the coast?

No one doubts that people from Siberia settled in the New World. But did some of the first Americans come from other places? If so, how did they travel? Did they survive or were they replaced by other peoples? If they survived, did they mix and mate with later arrivals?

The answers to these questions may well be found by still other scientists, by scientists who are not archaeologists.

A DECORATED SPEAR, PROBABLY OF MASTODON IVORY, WAS PRESERVED IN THE FRESH WATER OF A FLORIDA RIVER. IT WAS CARVED WHEN THE IVORY WAS FRESH. SINCE MASTODONS DIED OUT 13,000 YEARS AGO, THE CARVER MUST HAVE LIVED AT LEAST THAT LONG AGO.

CHAPTER FIVE

# SKULLS, LANGUAGES, & GENETICS

**T**HE BODY WAS FOUND BURIED IN A CAVE IN Nevada. The cave—named Spirit Cave—was so dry that part of the body had turned into a mummy. The remains were of a man 40 to 44 years old who was wrapped in a rabbit-skin blanket and wore leather moccasins. His body lay between two mats that had been sewn together. The mats had been woven of a marsh plant. They were so neatly woven that the people who made them must have had looms. Spirit Cave Man had some broken bones and a skull fracture that had partly healed. Scientists also saw infections in his gums.

When Spirit Cave Man was first found, scientists guessed he was about 2,000 years old. Carbon-14 dating corrected them. He was really 10,600 years old.

THIS UNOPENED BUNDLE CONTAINS THE REMAINS OF SPIRIT CAVE MAN, WHO LIVED 10,600 YEARS AGO. THE BLACK RECTANGLE COVERS A SMALL SPLIT THROUGH WHICH A FEW BONES CAN BE SEEN. AT THIS TIME, THE BONES OF SPIRIT CAVE MAN ARE NOT BEING SHOWN PUBLICLY. PARTS OF HIS LEATHER MOCCASINS WERE ALSO PRESERVED (ABOVE).

One of the many interesting things about him was the shape of his skull. He did not look like a Native American or a northern Asian. His skull was longer and narrower, his cheekbones smaller. His face was also shorter from the bridge of the nose to the upper lip.

Two anthropologists—Dr. Richard Jantz of the University of Tennessee and Dr. Douglas W. Owsley of the Smithsonian Institution—have spent years measuring the skulls of modern Native Americans in the Great Plains, Great Basin, and Southwest. By comparing measurements—65 for each skull—they can tell the members of one tribe from the members of another. When a Native American skeleton is discovered somewhere, they are often asked which tribe it should be returned to for burial. They have also studied old skulls.

Dr. Owsley says they were surprised by how different the older skulls were from any of the modern-day groups. Older skulls lacked the broad faces and big cheekbones seen in

THE UNDERLYING SKULL IN THE RECONSTRUCTIONS OF AN 830-YEAR-OLD NEVADA SKELETON (LEFT) IS MARKEDLY DIFFERENT FROM THAT OF SPIRIT CAVE MAN (RIGHT). THE DIFFERENCE IN SHAPE MAY MEAN THAT THEY DO NOT SHARE THE SAME ANCESTRY.

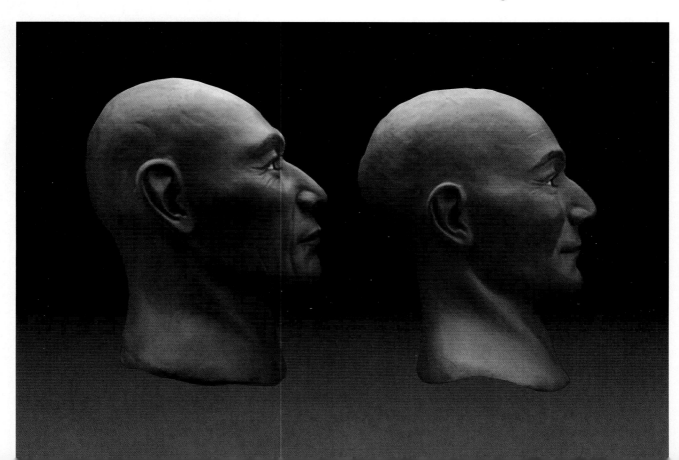

Northern Asians and in American Indians. Dr. Owsley says that skulls suddenly started to look like those of modern Native Americans only about 7,000 years ago.

The differences could mean that people from northeast Asia were not the earliest colonizers. They could even mean that some of the first colonizers were not ancestors of today's Native Americans.

A number of anthropologists think these ancient skulls look like those of modern Polynesians and of the Ainu, a people of northern Japan. The ancestors of the Ainu were hunter-gatherers who roamed coastal parts of Asia. Thousands of years ago—no one is sure when—they became the first settlers of Japan. Over time, the islands were invaded by the ancestors of the Japanese, who were rice growers, and the ancestors of the Ainu were driven north. Until the Ainu mixed with the Japanese, they looked very different from other Asian groups. They had longer heads, fair

ARROWS INDICATE SOME OF THE MOST IMPORTANT MEASUREMENTS THAT ANTHROPOLOGISTS MAKE WHEN MEASURING SKULLS.

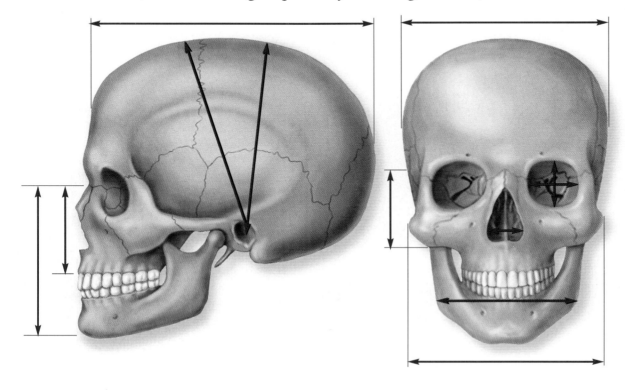

# COMPARING A FEW SKULLS

**10,600 YEARS OLD
SPIRIT CAVE MAN
NEVADA**

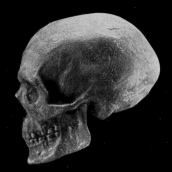

**9,500 YEARS OLD
KENNEWICK MAN
WASHINGTON**

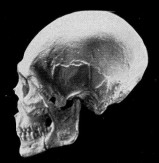

**MODERN AMERICAN INDIAN
GREAT PLAINS
NORTH AMERICA**

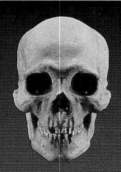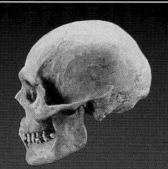

**MODERN EUROPEAN-
AMERICAN
NORTH AMERICA**

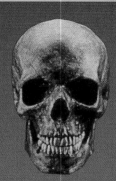

skin, wavy hair, thick beards, and, some early travelers reported, blue eyes.

South America also has skulls that do not look like those of modern American Indians. One is 13,500 years old — the oldest human remain found in the New World. The skull belonged to a young woman whom scientists named Luzia. Along with most of her skeleton, it was found buried in a cave at Lapa Vermelha, north of Rio de Janeiro, Brazil. Luzia stood a little less than five feet tall. She was part of a group of hunter-gatherers who seem to have lived mostly on whatever fruits, nuts, and berries they found. She died around age 20, after some sort of accident.

Luzia's skull looks nothing like those of today's American Indians. And it does not look like the ancient North American skulls. It looks, anthropologists say, like the skulls of Africans and of the Aborigines, the first people to live in Australia.

No anthropologist thinks Luzia or her ancestors reached South America from Africa or Australia. But some think she shares ancestors with the Aborigines. Among them is Dr. Walter Neves of the University of São Paulo, Brazil. He suggests that some of Luzia's ancestors moved through Southeast Asia to Java and Australia. Others traveled north along the coast of Asia, across the Bering Strait, and down the west coast of the Americas, perhaps 15,000 years ago.

Since Luzia was discovered, more than 40 other old skeletons have been found nearby in what appears to be a cemetery. Their skulls also look African. Scientists hope to learn much by studying them.

With only a small number of skulls to work with, anthropologists cannot be sure of where these people came from. Even so, some think that small groups of different peoples arrived in the New World at different times, and most

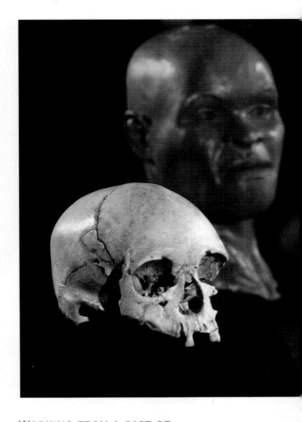

WORKING FROM A CAST OF LUZIA'S SKULL, A BRITISH SCULPTOR BUILT UP MUSCLES AND FLESH TO MAKE THIS RECONSTRUCTION OF WHAT THE YOUNG WOMAN MAY HAVE LOOKED LIKE.

DR. OWSLEY AND CONSERVATOR CAROLYN ROSE CLEAN AND STABILIZE THE SKULL OF A 10,000-YEAR-OLD WOMAN FOUND IN THE WESTERN UNITED STATES.

probably by different routes.

Another group of scientists has been studying the languages of Native Americans. These scientists are called linguists. A linguist may study how one language grew out of another or how different languages are related.

No one knows what language or languages the earliest Americans spoke. But modern Native American languages hold clues to the past. Some linguists have studied 150 language families native to the New World. None seem to be related to Old World languages. The linguists say it would take 30,000 years for people to develop that many languages. This, they say, shows that people have been in the Americas at least that long.

One linguist, Dr. Johanna Nichols of the University of California at Berkeley, thinks the languages spoken by the present-day Indians of North America grew out of those spoken by people in Central and South America. Her studies lead her to think that some languages formed around the Gulf of Mexico and the Caribbean. When people moved north, so did the languages. Perhaps, she says, Clovis people entered North America from South or Central America.

If this linguist is right, then the very first colonizers may have traveled down the west coast of the Americas and settled in Central and South America.

The science of genetics is also playing a part in the search for the first Americans. Genetics is the study of how traits are passed from one generation to another—of how they are inherited. It is the study of the genetic materials in plants, animals, and people. Some of the work now being done in genetics has to do with materials called mtDNA and Y chromosomes. This work is of great interest to scientists who are trying to track first Americans.

All of us carry mtDNA in nearly all the cells of our bodies. (Its full name is mitochondrial deoxyribonucleic acid.) Your mtDNA is a bit like a barcode that shows which large group of people you are related to. Your mtDNA pattern and theirs are similar.

MtDNA may be preserved in ancient bones. If it has been, tests will show which group of people the person belonged to.

MtDNA is inherited from only one parent, the mother. A child's mtDNA is usually exactly like its mother's. But sometimes a change, called a mutation, takes place. A woman passes on the change to her children. Over thousands of years there can be many mutations.

Nearly all Native American groups in the Americas carry one of four patterns of mtDNA. Three of the patterns are like those found in people of Siberia, but each shows changes found only in the Americas. This suggests that the ancestors of today's Siberians were also the ancestors of many Native Americans. The fourth pattern is not found in Siberia, but it is found elsewhere in Asia.

And this suggests that these ancestors did not pass through Siberia on their way to the Americas. It hints they may have taken a sea route.

Scientists can estimate the rate at which mutations take place. So they can tell how long ago the ancestors of two groups had the same mtDNA pattern. Sometimes they can tell where the ancestors lived.

Scientists work with Y chromosomes in much the same way. This genetic material is passed only from father to son. A son's Y chromosome is usually exactly like his father's. But on rare occasions a mutation takes place, and the change is passed on.

Genetic studies seem to show that early colonizers arrived in the New World from eastern Asia and Siberia about 35,000 to 25,000 years ago. That was well before the Ice Age reached its peak 21,000 years ago. More colonizers arrived after the glaciers started to melt and shrink. These were people who had been living in Beringia. They had lived there long enough to develop their own set of mutations.

Recently a fifth pattern was found in a few of today's Native Americans. The other four are found throughout the New World, but this one is found mostly in North America. It has not been found in East Asia or Siberia. But it has been found in European, Middle Eastern, and western Asian peoples. It seems to have arrived in the New World 30,000 to 15,000 years ago.

So far the fifth group is a mystery. No one knows where these people came from. Perhaps they were from Central Asia. Perhaps they moved from Europe to Asia to North America.

More genetic studies may solve the mystery. They may also show whether long-headed persons, such as Kennewick Man, are related to today's Native Americans.

# FINDING AN ANCIENT FACE

**T**his reconstruction of Spirit Cave Man's face used a cast of the skull. Over the years, scientists have worked out how thick a layer of flesh, or tissue, should be built on each part of the skull.

In the first step, tissue-depth markers were cut to the proper thickness and glued onto the cast.

In the second step, strips of oil-based clay were used to connect the markers.

In the third step, the eyes, nose, and mouth were blocked in.

In the final step, more clay was added and the face given human features that show how Spirit Cave Man may have looked when alive.

# THE SEARCH GOES ON

**F**OR MANY YEARS SCIENTISTS WENT TO PLACES where Indians lived or had lived, dug up graves, and carried off the contents for study at museums and universities. But they never asked the Indians if they might do this. In time, both scientists and other people came to see these actions as wrong. In 1990 Congress tried to give Native Americans control over the remains of their ancestors. It passed the Native American Graves Protection and Repatriation Act (NAGPRA).

NAGPRA says that if human remains are found on federal land, the government must find out if they are Native American. If they are, the remains must be given to a tribe they are related to. The same thing must happen if the scientific work is being supported by federal money.

THE SEARCH FOR EARLY AMERICANS LEADS SCIENTISTS TO MANY PLACES. DR. TIMOTHY HEATON (LEFT) WORKS IN A CRAMPED CAVE ON AN ISLAND IN SOUTHEAST ALASKA, WHERE HE HAS FOUND ANIMAL BONES WITH DATES SPANNING THE PAST 40,000 YEARS. THAT MEANS THE AREA WAS NOT BURIED UNDER GLACIERS BUT A PLACE WHERE ICE AGE PEOPLE COULD HAVE LIVED. ABOVE, TWO SCIENTISTS UNEARTH BONES AT A SITE IN FOLSOM, NEW MEXICO.

Kennewick Man was found on a piece of shoreline controlled by the United States Army Corps of Engineers. And so the remains came under NAGPRA.

Five tribes claimed the bones and wanted to bury them. These Indians believe that once a body goes into the ground, it is meant to stay there forever, to return to the earth, to become earth. They believe their Creator speaks to them through the land. One way for them to speak to their Creator is by returning to the land—to be buried and stay buried. The Indians also believe that they have been in the Americas since the beginning of time. And so they must be descendants of any very old remains found.

A group of scientists sued for the right to study the bones, saying that the government had not shown Kennewick Man was a Native American — or an ancestor of any tribe. If he wasn't, then NAGPRA would not apply. They also point out that if studies cannot be made of ancient bones, we will never learn how the Americas were first peopled. Much of what we know about early peoples has come from the study of their bones.

TWO ARCHAEOLOGISTS EXTRACT BONES FROM A MUDDY SITE AT ARCH LAKE, NEAR PORTALES, NEW MEXICO.

At the time of this writing, the bones of Kennewick Man were still in storage.

Today's scientists understand the need to find ways to work with tribes, to do science but also to respect religious beliefs. Some tribes and some scientists have managed to work together. Not all tribes share the same beliefs. Some permit studies, such as measurements, that do not change the remains. Some permit tests, such as carbon-14 dating, that destroy only a tiny amount of bone. Some scientists are good about talking with tribal groups, explaining their work, asking permission to make tests, sharing information so that the tribe learns more about its history.

Native Americans have feelings and beliefs that deserve to be respected. At the same time, if science is to move forward, scientists must be free to find things out.

Scientists long thought that the earliest colonizers arrived during a fairly brief time by crossing a land bridge. And so all Native Americans must be related. Now new discoveries are leading many to think that the Americas were settled over a long time by different types of people. More discoveries lie ahead and there are new theories to test.

One anthropologist, Dr. Robson Bonnichsen of the University of Oregon, has suggested, for example, that there were no Clovis people. Perhaps, he says, Clovis was a way of working stone, a technology. The technology spread as groups of people met to trade goods and look for mates. If Clovis was a technology, not a people, that would explain its rapid spread across North America.

Clovis spear points look very much like some from the Old World. Although people in far-flung parts of the world do invent the same things, some scientists wonder if Clovis stone-working techniques came from the Old World, perhaps from Ukraine. Similar tools and weapons have been found there, dating from 20,000 years ago.

Dr. Dennis Stanford, an archaeologist at the Smithsonian Institution, notes that Clovis

HER SEARCH HAS TAKEN DR. ROOSEVELT TO A PLACE WHERE NO SCIENTIST HAD EVER SET FOOT. TRAVELING BY SMALL PLANE AND BOAT, SHE REACHED A SITE DEEP IN THE AMAZON REGION OF BRAZIL, WHERE A GOLD PROSPECTOR HAD FOUND A LARGE POINT THAT DID NOT LOOK LIKE THOSE OF CLOVIS OR PEDRA PINTADA. IT IS OVAL, WITH SMALL BARBS ALONG ITS EDGES, WHICH SUGGESTS IT WAS USED FOR HARPOONING LARGE FISH. DR. ROOSEVELT, SHOWN HERE AFTER A DIVE IN AN AMAZON RIVER, IS EXPLORING UNDER-WATER IN THE KIND OF AREA WHERE ANCIENT PEOPLES WENT TO GATHER MATERIALS FOR TOOLS AND TO FISH.

PERHAPS BY CHANCE, A
20,000-YEAR-OLD STONE
POINT FROM NORTHERN SPAIN
(BELOW) LOOKS MUCH LIKE A
CLOVIS POINT.

working of stone and bone was very like the work done along the north coast of Spain 20,000 years ago. He wonders if people traveled by boat from Spain to the New World, following the edge of the pack ice that covered the North Atlantic during the Ice Age. If they did, it would explain why there are more Clovis sites in the southeastern United States than in the West. It would also explain why some of these sites appear to be older than the western sites. And it would explain why no link has been found between Clovis and the early people of Alaska.

Many scientists are doubtful that people could have crossed the Atlantic. Even if they followed the edge of the ice, there was no place to put ashore. Dr. Stanford agrees but says it is important to explore the possibility that Europeans were among the first Americans.

Others feel the same way. The idea also deserves exploring, they say, because we are always being surprised by what ancient peoples managed to do.

About 100,000 years ago, small bands of early modern humans set out from Africa. Traveling on foot, these remarkable people managed, over thousands of years, to settle every continent except Antarctica. The Americas were the last continents they reached.

When did they arrive? Where did they come from?

Not long ago, scientists thought they could answer these questions. Now new discoveries show that the mystery is not solved after all. The search for the first Americans goes on.

THE ROCK PAINTING AT RIGHT IS FROM RIO PINTURAS IN ARGENTINA.
THE CAVE PAINTINGS OF EUROPE ALSO SHOW HUMAN HANDS, PERHAPS
SAYING, "I WAS HERE."

# THE PEOPLING OF THE AMERICAS

**T**he earliest humans to reach the Americas may have come by land or by sea or by land and sea. The different routes they may have taken are shown on this map.

The blue arrows on top of the ice show where there was a passageway both before the two great glaciers came together and after they began to melt and shrink back. The passageway was closed for thousands of years during the height of the Ice Age.

It seems likely that the chief migration of people to the Americas took place once the ice had melted back. Many were people who had been living on the Bering Land Bridge and had moved there from Siberia.

ARTWORK IN THE CAVE AT MONTE ALEGRE IN BRAZIL WAS KNOWN TO LOCAL PEOPLE AND LED DR. ROOSEVELT TO SEARCH FOR TRACES OF EARLY HUNTERS.

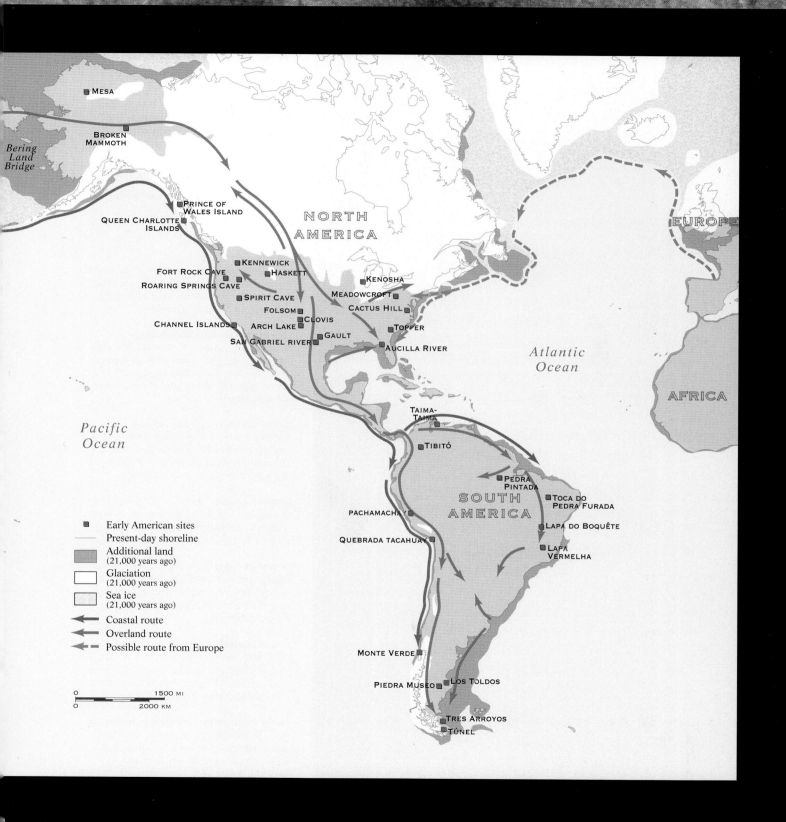

MESA

BROKEN
MAMMOTH

Bering
Land
Bridge

PRINCE OF
WALES ISLAND

QUEEN CHARLOTTE
ISLANDS

NORTH
AMERICA

EUROPE

KENNEWICK

FORT ROCK CAVE

HASKETT

ROARING SPRINGS CAVE

KENOSHA

SPIRIT CAVE

MEADOWCROFT

FOLSOM

CACTUS HILL

CHANNEL ISLANDS

CLOVIS

ARCH LAKE

TOPPER

SAN GABRIEL RIVER

GAULT

AUCILLA RIVER

Atlantic
Ocean

AFRICA

Pacific
Ocean

TAIMA-
TAIMA

TIBITÓ

PEDRA
PINTADA

TOCA DO
PEDRA FURADA

PACHAMACHAY

SOUTH
AMERICA

LAPA DO BOQUÊTE

QUEBRADA TACAHUAY

LAPA
VERMELHA

■ Early American sites

—— Present-day shoreline

Additional land
(21,000 years ago)

Glaciation
(21,000 years ago)

Sea ice
(21,000 years ago)

→ Coastal route

→ Overland route

⇢ Possible route from Europe

MONTE VERDE

PIEDRA MUSEO

LOS TOLDOS

0          1500 MI

0          2000 KM

TRES ARROYOS

TÚNEL

# C H R O N O L O G Y

| Number of Calendar Years Ago | Event or Settlement |
|---|---|
| 35,000 – 25,000* | Possible early migration to the American continents. |
| 21,000 | Height of the Ice Age. Glaciers meet, closing corridor through Canada. |
| 20,000 | People in southwestern Europe and Ukraine make tools similar to Clovis tools. |
| 20,000* | Meadowcroft settlement in the eastern United States. |
| 18,000* | Cactus Hill settlement in the eastern United States. |
| 14,800* | Monte Verde settlement in Chile. |
| 14,000 | Broken Mammoth settlement in Alaska. |
| 13,500 | Clovis settlements in the southwestern United States. |
| 13,500 | Pedra Pintada settlement in eastern Brazil. |
| 13,500* | The skull of Luzia, found in Brazil. |
| 12,500 | Folsom settlements in the southwestern United States. |
| 11,000 | Ice Age ends. Glaciers are melting and shrinking apart. |
| 10,600 | Spirit Cave Man. |
| 9,500 | Kennewick Man. |

*indicates date not accepted by all*

# RESOURCES

## FURTHER READING

*Dig.* A magazine for kids 8 to 13 that covers the excitement, mystery, and fun of archaeology, paleontology, and earth science. Published in cooperation with the Archaeological Institute of America. Six issues per year. Cobblestone Publishing Company, 30 Grove Street, Suite C, Peterborough, NH 03458; 1-800-821-0115; www.digonsite.com

## WEB SITES

**emuseum.mnsu.edu**—Offers information on archaeology, anthropology, cultures, prehistory, and more. Maintained by Minnesota State University.

**www.archaeology.about.com**—Contains a variety of information on archaeology, including a list of current digs all over the world sponsored by universities that are open to students or volunteers.

**www.archaeologychannel.org**—Offers short videos about archaeological digs and expeditions. You need a Windows media player or a RealPlayer on your computer to see them.

**www.digonsite.com**—Web site of the magazine *Dig.* Contains a state-by-state guide to archaeology and paleontology events for kids, families, and schools.

**www.friendsofpast.org**—Offers news and comment on Kennewick Man and other ancient remains and on protecting the rights of Americans to learn about prehistory.

**www.centerfirstamericans.com**—This site has just been moved to Texas A&M University and is currently being redesigned. Of special interest is the "Breaking News" section.

**www.questorsys.com/rockart/links.htm**—Contains much information about rock art and lists rock art sites that can be visited in all parts of the world.

www.uiowa.edu/~osa/nasa—Site of the National Association of State Archaeologists. Contains a list of all state archaeologists, who can be contacted for more information about sites and archaeology in their states.

//archnet.asu.edu/—Contains a list of museums, exhibits, and Internet sites about archaeology. Sponsored by the Archaeological Research Institute at Arizona State University.

With a search engine, you can find many other web sites, especially state web sites, under the subject heading "prehistoric Americans."

### VIDEO

*In Search of History: The First Americans.* Examines the latest theories, and some of the discredited ones, surrounding the arrival of people in the new world. 50 minutes. #AAE42398. A&E Television. www.aande.com

### SELECTED BIBLIOGRAPHY

Adovasio, J. M. with Jake Page. *The First Americans: In Pursuit of Archaeology's Greatest Mystery.* New York: Random House, 2002.

Cavalli-Sforza, Luigi Luca. *Genes, Peoples and Languages.* Translated by Mark Seielstad. New York: North Point Press/Farrar, Straus & Giroux, 2000.

Chatters, James C. *Ancient Encounters: Kennewick Man and the First Americans.* New York: Simon & Schuster, 2001.

Dillehay, Thomas D. *The Settlement of the Americas: A New Prehistory.* New York: Basic Books, 2000.

Jones, Martin. *The Molecule Hunt: Archaeology and the Search for Ancient DNA.* New York: Arcade Publishing, 2002.

Malcomson, Scott L. "The Color of Bones." The *New York Times Magazine*, April 2, 2000.

Olsen, Steve. *Mapping Human History: Discovering the Past Through Our Genes.* Boston: Houghton Mifflin, 2002.

Parfit, Michael. "Hunt for the First Americans." *National Geographic*, December 2000.

Preston, Douglas. "The Lost Man." *New Yorker*, June 16, 1997.

*Scientific American Discovering Archaeology*, January/February 2000. Special report: "The Puzzle of the First Americans."

Thomas, David Hurst. *Skull Wars: Kennewick Man, Archaeology, and the Battle for Native American Identity.* New York: Basic Books, 2000.

Cover: (Background) A.C. Roosevelt, Courtesy of The Field Museum, Chicago; (skull) Doug Owsley, photography by Chip Clark, NMNH, Smithsonian Institution; (left) Matthew Frey; (center, left) Matthew Frey; (center, right), Ramulo Fiandini, Courtesy of Museu Goeldi, Banco Safra; (right) Matthew Frey.

1 (skull), Doug Owsley, photography by Chip Clark, NMNH, Smithsonian Institution; 1 (background), ©1993 Photo by A.C. Roosevelt, Courtesy of The Field Museum, Chicago; 3, 1993 Photo by Ramulo Fiandini, Courtesy of Museu Goeldi, Banco Safra; 4 (inset), James C. Chatters; 4 (background), A.C. Roosevelt, Courtesy of The Field Museum, Chicago; 5 (upper), Matthew Frey; 5 (lower), James C. Chatters; 6 (both), James C. Chatters; 7, Steve Harrison; 8, Gregory A. Harlin; 9, Ramulo Fiandini, Courtesy of Museu Goeldi, Banco Safra; 10 (background), A.C. Roosevelt, Courtesy of The Field Museum, Chicago; 10 (inset), Theodor de Bry/The Mariners' Museum/CORBIS; 11 (upper), Matthew Frey; 11 (lower), Theodor de Bry/CORBIS; 12, Tibor G. Toth; 12-13, David Alan Harvey; 14 (left), Richard Schlecht; 14 (right), Kenneth Garrett; 16, J.M. Adovasio, Courtesy Mercyhurst Archaeological Institute; 17 (upper, both), Kenneth Garrett; 17 (lower), Peter A. Bostrom; 18, Gregory A. Harlin; 19 (upper), Illustrations by Eric Parrish, from *Bones, Boats & Bison*, 1999:153; 19 (lower), Peter A. Bostrom; 20-21, Tom Wolff; 21, David L. Arnold; 22, Peter A. Bostrom; 24-25, Kenneth Garrett; 26 (background), A.C. Roosevelt, Courtesy of The Field Museum, Chicago; 26 (inset), Kenneth Garrett; 27 (lower), Kenneth Garrett; 27 (upper), Matthew Frey; 28 (upper), Tom D. Dillehay; 28 (lower, all), Kenneth Garrett; 29, Richard Schlecht; 31 (left), Gregory A. Harlin; 31 (right), Kenneth Garrett; 32, Diego Goldberg, Courtesy of The Field Museum, Chicago; 32-33 (upper), A.C. Roosevelt, Courtesy of The Field Museum, Chicago; 32-33 (lower), Romulo Findini, Courtesy of The Field Museum, Chicago; 33 (lower), Diego Goldberg, Courtesy of The Field Museum, Chicago; 35, Kenneth Garrett; 36 (background), A.C. Roosevelt, Courtesy of The Field Museum, Chicago; 36 (inset), Kenneth Garrett; 37 (upper), Matthew Frey; 37 (lower), J.M. Adovasio, Courtesy Mercyhurst Archaeological Institute; 39 (upper), Kenneth Garrett; 39 (lower), Matthew Frey; 40, Richard Schlecht; 42, Tom D. Dillehay; 43, Kenneth Garrett; 44, Doug Owsley, photography by Chip Clark, Courtesy NMNH, Smithsonian Institution; 45 (upper), Matthew Frey; 45 (lower), Nevada State Museum; 46, Doug Owsley, photography by Chip Clark, NMNH, Smithsonian Institution; 48, Doug Owsley, photography by Chip Clark, NMNH, Smithsonian Institution; 49, Greg Newton/Reuters/CORBIS; 50, Doug Owsley, photography by Chip Clark, NMNH, Smithsonian Institution; 53 (upper), Keith Kasnot; 53 (center), Doug Owsley, photography by Chip Clark, Courtesy Nevada State Museum; 53 (lower), Doug Owsley, photography by Chip Clark, NMNH, Smithsonian Institution; 54 (inset), Kenneth Garrett; 54 (background), A.C. Roosevelt, Courtesy of The Field Museum, Chicago; 55 (both), Kenneth Garrett; 56, Kenneth Garrett; 57, John Dorfman; 58, Chip Clark, Courtesy NMNH, Smithsonian Institution; 59, James P. Blair; 60 (upper), Kenneth Garrett; 60 (lower), A.C. Roosevelt, The Field Museum, Chicago; 60-61 (background), A.C. Roosevelt, Courtesy of The Field Museum, Chicago; 63, Peter A. Bostrom.

NMNH - National Museum of Natural History

One of the world's largest nonprofit scientific and educational organizations, the National Geographic Society was founded in 1888 "for the increase and diffusion of geographic knowledge." Fulfilling this mission, the Society educates and inspires millions every day through its magazines, books, television programs, videos, maps and atlases, research grants, the National Geographic Bee, teacher workshops, and innovative classroom materials. The Society is supported through membership dues, charitable gifts, and income from the sale of its educational products. This support is vital to National Geographic's mission to increase global understanding and promote conservation of our planet through exploration, research, and education.

For more information, please call
1-800-NGS-LINE (647-5463) or write to the following address:
National Geographic Society
1145 17th Street N.W.
Washington, D.C. 20036-4688
U.S.A.

Visit the Society's Web site: www.nationalgeographic.com